A Step by Step Concierge Handbook

CONCIERGE AND LIFESTYLE
MANAGER MANUAL

A Step by Step Concierge Handbook

CONCIERGE AND LIFESTYLE MANAGER MANUAL

IV EDITION

Revised by Suzanne Jones

Manager of Concierge Services

CONCIERGE AND LIFESTYLE MANAGER MANUAL

978-0-615-16585-1

Table of Contents

STARTING A CONCIERGE SERVICE

Contact Us

CONCIERGE AND LIFESTYLE MANAGER MANUAL

CONCIERGE AND LIFESTYLE

MANAGERS IN THE 21ST CENTURY

A CAREER YOU CAN DO ANYWHERE…
Start Your Own Concierge/ Lifestyle
Management Company from home or
anywhere in the world
Anyone can do it…Anywhere
The business that can go anywhere you go.
All you need is an iPad or laptop, cell phone;
blue tooth technology, a savvy and
professional style, organizational skills and
you are on your way.
A career you can do anywhere…

Desiree Ertuly

L

CONCIERGE AND LIFESTYLE MANAGER MANUAL

Start a Concierge Lifestyle Management Company the business trend of today.

A sure way to succeed in the concierge business is to follow a plan.
The author has illustrated her plan of action in this book. The Manual is an easy step by step guide to a successful business…

- Develop a burning desire for the business you want to implement
- Daily Affirmations or Confessions of faith
- Believe you will succeed and you will
- Build Confidence and eradicate fear
- Goal set (Project Management is essential)
- Develop a business plan and follow it (if the plan is not working revise it)
- Focus on one business at a time
- Look important (When you look good, you feel good, and when you feel good you perform great) quote from Yadah Yadah
- Develop love and gratefulness
- Just do it! (Nike motto)

Black car service around the globe...

What is a concierge?

A concierge is a gatekeeper, a keeper of the keys to busy households. The concierge business specializes in personal assistant, chauffeur service, household management service, errands, relocation specialist, arrange for the butler, and housekeeper. A concierge does event planning, travel planning, finding the hard to find items, and so much more.

You can find a concierge in commercial office buildings, private clubs, luxury condominiums, luxury residential communities, private companies, airports, associations, malls, and hospitals. You can find concierge services in a kiosk with database integration it is a trend in hotels, the mall; you can put a kiosk in a hospital, or at the airport.

There are many places and ways to start a concierge business. Choose one at a time then you will become an expert. You can cater to medical professionals only, doctors and nurses who are extremely busy professionals; the affluent individuals only, elderly, or professional athletes. The concierge services are designed for busy professionals and anyone who need more time in a day. As a concierge you become your clients "to do list" specialist. A great tool to possess is an iPad and blackberry device.

A concierge develops relationships with companies and professionals. As a concierge you must be resourceful and be able to get VIP seats at exclusive clubs and restaurants, charter a jet, reserve a limousine or black car service anywhere; arrange a vacation where beauty and elegance blend with an exotic and an exciting experience. Upscale concierge companies assist clients in making the impossible, become possible.

A concierge provider can charge by membership or a' la Carte. See our membership plans we offer in the samples later in the book.

You can set the business up as a:

CONCIERGE AND LIFESTYLE MANAGER MANUAL

Corporate Concierge
Private Concierge
Personal Concierge
Lifestyle Planner
Lifestyle Management Company
Personal Assistant

What is a Personal Assistant? What is a Celebrity Personal Assistant or Lifestyle Manager?

Lifestyle Manager or Personal Assistant is pretty much the same. Some lifestyle management companies are similar to Upscale Lifestyle Concierge. The company does not run errands.

A lifestyle manager or celebrity personal assistant take on the role of a Publicist; assist with marketing the celebrity, branding the client image, screening fan mail, answering phones, sending out blast emails, setting up Facebook and Twitter accounts, and planning parties.

Concierge, lifestyle managers, and personal assistants are allowed to enter a private world and live like celebrities. A client may need you to travel for business. Who says you can't travel for business as well as pleasure.

Remember busy professionals, celebrities, novelist, professional athletes, and CEO's need groceries, need to schedule doctor's appointments, and acquire rest just like everyone else. However, unlike everyone else these busy professionals also have to be in the studio preparing for their next hit record deal. The clients need to do movie shoots, and attend important meetings. The celebrity must practice their profession. The celebrity assistant makes volumes of phone calls for the celebrity, read and respond to emails, in some cases read and update Facebook and Twitter. The lifestyle manager/ celebrity personal assistant makes sure that everything gets done, allowing the celebrity **Time** to enjoy their life. Upscale Lifestyle Concierge Motto is "Making your life more enjoyable."™ A savvy lifestyle manager/celebrity personal assistant functions as a coordinator, a friend, and a planner. The lifestyle manager offers anything and everything that an affluent client requires. (As long as the requirement is legal and ethical) The personal assistant/lifestyle manager offers the client organization and peace of mind.

Perks of the business may

- A great compensation, first class travel, VIP passes into nightclubs with your client, expensive gifts, and an extended network.

There are six figure salary lifestyle managers because the client requires a college degree. For example here is a request from a potential client.

All candidates must have:

-24/7 availability

-Strong MS Office skills

-Superior communication skills (both written and verbal)

-At least 5 years' experience working as an Executive Assistant/Personal Assistant

-Experience working for a high level executive (C-Level and above)

-Ability to travel

- Must have a Bachelor's Degree

-Must have experience as a lifestyle manager/personal assistant

-Must be flexible with hours

-Knowledge of French is a plus

Computer literacy is required you should be able to successfully navigate across multiple applications simultaneously including Yahoo, Google, or Bing, Internet Explorer, Google Chrome, MS Word, Excel, and Outlook. One must acquire computer skills, become internet savvy, take a sales course, or a business course to brush up on your business and personal etiquette skills.

For a client that purchase a yacht excursion a lifestyle manager can charge the vendor a percentage for referral and the client for the service request.

CONCIERGE AND LIFESTYLE MANAGER MANUAL

If a client wants an exotic coffee or special bean from Africa, an hourly fee can be administered to find the hard to find. Does this sound like a great business to you? If so, you may have found the part of the lifestyle management business that suits you.

As a celebrity personal assistant, you can earn over $100,000 per year, and enjoy an amazing lifestyle that most people will only dream about. A formal education is not necessary to do this business; but if you have a formal education, education this will give you more leverage in the business. Skills and traits of a lifestyle manager are a refined appearance, integrity, and a great personality. Critical thinking skills are essential for the success of the concierge and lifestyle management business. One becomes a problem solver using creativity for some clients. Sometime you may have to work 24 hour days in the beginning to get the business going in a positive direction.

As a professional in this industry you must be organized. You must handle this business with confidentiality it is vital to use discretion when dealing with clients of this caliber. You must be consistent and persistent to achieve the goals you commit to paper. With today's technology, anyone can get organized.

Microsoft Outlook, Project and my Blackberry device are my friends. My daily to do list is created using the software also, weekly planner, contact list, and an address book.

Sample

Things to do list

Short term goal

Mail vendor agreements and letters to

Lifestyle management companies for networking relationships

Follow up call for the businesses and confirm the affiliates received the package sent

Research the culture and values of the company in which we will do business with.

Contract business to concierge provider for client in Canada

Send letters to potential clients

Place ad on Career Builder job board
Send blast email every Thursday
Form an alliance with Hawaiian airlines
Go to meetup in New York tonight to network
Black car service for Mr. Jones 3 pm Thursday to the airport
Hotel reservation for Ann Wed Jun 3rd- 7th

In using the Microsoft Outlook, you can check off the task you have completed.

Don't procrastinate start your business now!
Start your concierge business now!
To get started ask yourself the following questions:
Do you have a passion for this type of business? If you have a passion for working with affluent people from all countries, you can and will succeed in this business.
How strong is your motivation to succeed in your home-based Concierge and lifestyle management business? If you answer this question with I can and I will succeed in this business, you are on your way.
Do you like the idea of controlling your day or would you rather let someone else be in command of your day?
If you want to empower others, you must empower yourself. Taking the risk of controlling your own life is commendable. Are you ready to work smarter and harder than you ever worked?
A day in the life of the business could be you answering all the calls, and then running two or three errands, typing several letters for a celebrity, screening fan mail and research of an exotic coffee in Africa. The example is more than 24 hours of work. Some days the concierge service is more exciting, booking a limousine reservation for a business traveler, making a reservation for hotel accommodation in a luxury suite, going shopping, and to lunch with your client. If you can handle this in a smart way, then keep reading.

CONCIERGE AND LIFESTYLE MANAGER MANUAL

-How will you develop a strong network of potential customers? Chamber of Commerce is a good networking organization, (BNI) Business leader meetings are lucrative, online business groups and Toastmasters is great for networking. Meetups in New York, Miami, DC and other areas are very good for this business. Join social and hobby groups on Meetups you will become motivated with the results. Networking definitely has its advantages.

-Have you set a goal or written a plan for making the transition into your new business? This is a very important step.

-Do you have any money saved that can get you over the small beginning stage of your business? When I started I acquired a loan for 10k to start my business. The money was used for a living allowance, a new laptop, and a cellular device, office equipment such as a fax machine, a mobile HP mini printer, Blackberry technology, a website, toll free number and educational material.

While on the go I am in my car texting; I am in my car 50% of the time. (Pull over to the side of the road to reply to clients) I meet clients at Starbucks, Panera's Bread, and sometime at their home or mine. These are hot spots for wireless access and very nice business comfortable atmospheres. Can you see how important the laptop, mini mobile printer, eFax and an excellent phone is to this business?

-Do you have self-confidence?

Developing this skill is crucial in this business; you must know your self-worth or you will feel very small dealing with the client in this industry. Never depreciate your worth.

-Do you have family support? Strong support teams keep the stress to a minimum, if your family members are in favor with whatever makes you happy. Having the support, you need when starting a business is a strong key to your success. I have the best daughters in the world. My daughters support me in any and every endeavor. I am their strong support team also. If you don't have a support team, it can hinder your creativity.

-Do you have customer service skills and a positive outlook on life? In today's market for business, service is imperative for the survival of any business. Show me a service-oriented company, I will show you a successful company.

-Are you able to keep your current employment while starting your business? The load is lighter when you have money coming in to handle the expense of a new start-up business. If you answered, the following questions positively continue to read.

Starting a business is a journey that requires many small steps to achieve the ultimate outcome success.

What is a home based business?

A home based business a small step in a positive direction eliminates the expense of an office or even a large corporation.

A home based business is simply a business started in your home. I started the business in a three bedroom apartment. In which I used one room as an office. In the apartment, the spare room was used as an office. The office was great until a family member needed a place to live for a few months. Consequently, my business was forced into the kitchen; my desk was the kitchen table. I tried working in the bedroom; the bedroom was not a good idea. The bedroom is for rest and not works. The table worked until I moved into a big house.

If you are starting from scratch, you may want to hone the skills you have developed over the years to avoid procrastination, and get started. If you start a class or course works at a college or a university, do not waste time, just learning. Apply a steady application of what you are learning into your business.

A good book to read is "The Complete Idiot's Guide to Etiquette," by Mary Mitchell with John Corr. In creating a new and exciting career in lifestyle management and concierge read everything you can on the

CONCIERGE AND LIFESTYLE MANAGER MANUAL

type of clients you will be working with. Observe at least 100 successful concierge and lifestyle management companies to see what each one does. Read magazines such as Conde Naste, Trends, and Robb Report, Luxury Lifestyle, Forbes, Fine Living, and Fortune magazine and wealth conscious books to motivate you toward your career as a business owner. Books that have developed my success are, "Think and Grow Rich by Napoleon Hill, Rich Dad Poor Dad by Robert T. Kiyosaki, The Magic of thinking BIG by Dr. Schwartz, Make every contact count and Professional image" these books have been my guiding mentors. I have read every article written about Mary Naylor the founder of VIP desk out of Virginia. She is positively one of my mentors and I have not met her yet. I have read some articles on line about VIP desk that indicate the company had an amazing growth rate compared to other concierge services offering the type of service her company offers.

Chose the services you would like to offer. Your list does not have to be lengthy. There is a wealth of information on the world-wide web.
Write down your talents. Writing your talents down will give you insight on the services you want to offer. Your talents you have written are your strengths. You have mastered these talents therefore; you can offer distinction and expertise in the services you chose. Your talent can bring you great rewards financially and psychologically.

Write your mission statement.
Your personal mission statement will help you to develop a mission statement for your business. Also, you will realize the difference in your life as you continue moving toward the business. You will see your mission unfold as you continuously look at your mission statement on a consistent basis.

Plan of action
When you follow the plan, you will succeed.

Step 1 Write your mission statement.
Upscale Lifestyle Concierge & Lifestyle
Management statement:
The company mission is to exceed our client's expectation
by providing a world-class service.
Our company is built on the principles of providing reliable
service.
Our cutting-edge service continues to grow by following
trends, improving our standard services and listening to the
client.
Our unique personalized service has established our place
in the lifestyle management industry. This allows us to make
a distinctive and substantial impact for our clients.
To be profitable by providing more than we receive (going
above and beyond)

Step 2 Select a business structure and occupational
business license contingent on the Geographic's of your
company. Most cities require a business license to do
business.
There are advantages and disadvantages in each ownership
structure.
There are for basic business structures I will discuss
business structures
  1. Sole Proprietorship
  2. Partnership
  3. Limited Liability Companies
  4. Corporation
Sole Proprietorship essentially is the simplest and common
form of business ownership. In essence the business and
the business owner are totally connected.
The sole proprietorship is usually managed by one person.

CONCIERGE AND LIFESTYLE MANAGER MANUAL

Advantage is the sole proprietorship is easy to establish and terminate. The sole proprietor makes all the decisions, there is no one to agree or disagree with the decisions you make. The owner is in total control of the business. The excitement of being your own boss is a plus, pride of ownership, retention of profits, and no special tax; you pay normal tax on this structure. There are tax advantages to business ownership. The business, or part of it, can be sold, altered, sold, or exchanged at will.

The disadvantage is unlimited liability, all debts and damages fall on the sole proprietorship. Creditors may seize personal as well as business property in settlement of debts. Limited financial resource is another disadvantage, all expense and expenditures fall on the individual.

When choosing this structure make sure you insure yourself with a business liability insurance policy. Make sure you have available resources. Another disadvantage is the lack of skills to handle every area of the business.

You may have customer service and selling skills, but what about accounting, legal skills, and managing people skills these are all necessary for a good business.

Limiting growth factors, you need people for creativity, for skills you lack, and the overwhelming commitment of being in too many places at one time. Team work is essential in building a business. Find a system that works for your company. Contracting service providers with insurance is essential in this business.

Partnership is a legal form with two or more owners. Advantage of this legal form is shared profits and loss. Partnerships the owner's shares operating the business, the partners share obligations of assuming liabilities. The partner share knowledge and skills of operating the business. Disadvantage is like the sole proprietorship owners totally liable for all debts. Should any partner neglect their obligations, the other partner can be forced to pay.

A popular business structure is the Limited Liability Partnership (LLP) the partners are not responsible for the businesses debt beyond the amount of their investment in the organization. The partner's personal assets are not at risk.

Advantage of Partnership is there are more financial resources to work with. A fact is when two or more people pool their resources the more the business can grow. Another advantage is shared management and more collective knowledge. Partnership is definitely easier to do the day-to day business and free up time for the other partner to get other things completed. Disadvantage is like sole proprietorship a general partnership could cause a partner to lose their house, cars, and anything else to debt. To avoid this disadvantage find the rights partners and form a LLP. Disagreements among partners about money, authority, and other conflicts are many. To deter this disadvantage spell out everything you can think of in writing to avoid and protect all involved. Last but not least, the partnership structure is difficult to terminate. When the business has grown dividing assets and profits are difficult. Breaking up may be hard to do, much like a marriage. Write out the particulars up front in a partnership agreement.

A Corporation is an artificial entity that really only exists in the eyes of the law. Corporations are legal entities formed under the laws of the state in which they are created. Corporations conduct business as a legal person which can enter into contracts, pay taxes, hire staff, file lawsuits, borrow money, and raise money by issuing stocks.

A (C) Corporation is a conventional state chartered entity with power to have liability separate from the owners. The owner is not liable for any debt incurred by the corporation beyond the money the stockholder invests. The corporation owners are stockholders. Owners do not have to worry about losing their house, their cars, or any other personal assets. The corporation offers a significant benefit to the owner. Significant advantage is more money to invest in the business is the main advantage of corporations. To raise capital, corporations sell ownership (stock) to anyone who is interested in owning a part of the business. Example GM sells a share for $50 each and you buy 10 million shares, the company will have 500 million dollars to buy materials, hire people, market, Research & Development and so much more. Advantage is limited liability for debts and actions of the corporation. Disadvantage it is generally the most costly to organize and maintain. State and federal regulations of corporation can be excessive. S Corporation advantage it has all the benefits of a corporation, plus a different method of taxation. Advantage is no double taxation. Size is an advantage with many owners or shareholders you can purchase large office buildings, invest in real-estate, and owners can take advantage of opportunities anywhere in the world. Perpetual life, a corporation does not die because an owner dies. Easy to change ownership, if you don't want to be a part of the corporation all you have to do is sell your stock to someone else. With this form, you can hire the best employees because you have leverage to offer the benefits and perks of a large corporation, stock options and the pay to stay. Also, your employees can buy ownership into the business buying shares at a discount.

Disadvantage of the corporation is the initial cost the lawyers, accountants, and the cost of paperwork. Paperwork can be a headache. Tax laws place a demand on owners to prove all of the company's expenses to make sure the expenses, deductions, and tax breaks are legitimate. A corporation must keep detailed records of the minutes taken at the meetings and more. The owner that files the corporation must file two tax forms an individual and corporation form.

The corporate return can be difficult to file that is why you will need to hire an accountant. The size can be an advantage and a disadvantage; with large corporations, it can be hard to change quickly with the trends. Sometime all the legalities and red tape associated with laws can hinder the changes necessary for a large corporation to keep up with the trends. Corporations are very difficult entities to terminate. Corporations are double taxed. The corporation has to pay tax on the income before it can distribute dividends to stockholders. Then the stockholders have to pay tax on the dividends.

A disadvantage can be a conflict with the board of directors. The owner can be forced out of the company he founded. Since the board of directors make decisions on who should be the officers of the company. S Corp is not recommended by organization because it looks like a corporation but it is taxed like a sole proprietorship and general partnership.

The next advantage is limited liability companies. Many companies in England have Ltd on the end of their name, it stands for limited liability, and the key here is the owner is only responsible for the losses up to the amount they invest. Limited Liability Companies are very similar to partnerships and are treated as sole proprietorships, partnerships, or corporations for the reporting of income and the payment of taxes. Their primary benefits are: Regulations covering formation and operation are generally easier. The members are protected against the companies' liability for debt and negligence.

The business structure is very important you cannot avoid step 2 in starting your concierge/lifestyle management business.
The step is simplified so anyone can understand it.

Step 3 Find a lawyer (A lawyer to look over your vendor agreements, also you can get clients from the lawyer and from their clients.) Vendor agreements are sold by my company for as low as $150 per form. A new and savvy inexpensive legal entity is prepaid lawyers; you pay a monthly fee, and they look over documents and give legal advice.

Step 4 Find an accountant many sole proprietors and partnerships use QuickBooks one must be diligent using QuickBooks record everything, it will be advantageous to you when it comes to audits and accounting for taxes.

CONCIERGE AND LIFESTYLE MANAGER MANUAL

Step 5 Find an insurance company for insurance and bonding get insurance up to $1,000,000 policy for a concierge company in Florida which a liability policy cost 300.00 annually.

Step 6 Choose a name (while researching the market don't take too long to get started it leads to procrastination) It's all in a name we have a name expert if you can't think of a catchy name call us 888-511-1887 ext. 80.
A logo designer expert created Upscale Lifestyle Concierge logo for 100.00

Step 7 Write a business plan. Now that you know what business legal structure you will use, you need a strategic plan. The plan is like a bible, the business plan is the direction your business going in. If you are conservative and do not want the hectic life of celebrities, you may start a personal concierge business for busy people, not necessarily wealthy people but middle class. See my sample plan; also, you may want to apply for a loan, when applying for a loan you will need a business plan. Upscale Lifestyle will do your business plan for 199.
See the business plan at the end of this book

Step 8 Develop a Vendor list (create favorites or bookmarks on the internet) Send a contractor letter to all vendors with an agreement. Vendors are needed (make a list of favorites and organize into folders so when the calls come in you are prepared to go to the worldwide list of vendors you have researched. Initial contact can be via email and then mail a letter to the prospective vendors. The easy way to do your vendor list is to put a keyword example: Flowers on the search engine you will get large list of local and world-wide vendors. Make the top vendors your favorites and make a contact with the vendor to network business referrals.

Step 9 Set up your Client database. CRM is trending. However, when we started we used software we purchased from eBay. The software is called My Database by My Software. The software can be customized for your company. You can also use a database you create in Microsoft Access or you can order a database called Tritrax from Triangle. Also, a company called Client Ease have database you can use on the go.

Here are some of the fields you want in your database:

Account Number
Client Name
Title
Company
Business Type
Email Address
Work Address
City State
Zip Code
Phone (work)
Phone (home)
Fax
Client Birthday
Single/Married Spouse's Name
Age Range
How does client contact you?
 Phone
 Fax
 E-mail

Step 10 Have a client and vendor contract list before implementing the business. An agreement is very important. An agreement can save you from a law suit and legal problems should your vendor fail to give the client the level of excellence you promised. With an agreement, the contract let your client know you use vendors from time to time. A contract lets your vendor know that their company is responsible for all claims, damages and unsatisfactory

CONCIERGE AND LIFESTYLE MANAGER MANUAL

complaints. The contract also let the vendor know the contract will be terminated for poor service and quality standards. Upscale Lifestyle Concierge sell both contracts for $250, you can sit with an attorney and add or take away some of the legal language Upscale Lifestyle Concierge use.

Step 11 Research local and world-wide competitors… Research we researched the business here is the market analysis of the segment Upscale Lifestyle Concierge market to, you may want to consider this market for your company. See a profile segment of Upscale Lifestyle client profile and market research

Customer Profile: Affluent individuals worldwide visiting Orlando, Miami, Atlanta and New York

Age: baby boomers (spend on personal services)

Gender: Women, Men

Location: World-Wide

Income level: combined family $500k +

Social class and occupation: higher education, CEO's, clergies, celebrities, affluent professionals

Education: Undergraduate degree, Graduate degree

For business customers, the demographic factors are:

Industry (or portion of an industry)

 All industries

Location World-wide

Size of firm 50 employees or more

The website has the greatest potential for the largest revenue for concierge clients. The typical user of the Internet is well educated and affluent. According to e-Market in 2010, 898 million users between the age of 35 and 64 were online in the United States. The age group accounts for 51% of the population by 2012

2011 $3.3 trillion dollars was spent on products and services. The staggering numbers on the rise these numbers lets the concierge business know the internet is a great media to target the majority of potential clients. Currently, there are over 1, 938,710,929 people using the Internet internationally. Sixty-nine percent of the online population has made at least one purchase in the last 90 days.

By 2017, over half of the world households will be online shopping.

According to the January 2009 Trend/Forecasting report of The Dilenschneider Group, in the U.S. alone, the 2009 holiday season online shopping jumped by more than 25% from 2005. (Note we are in a recession)

The average income of Internet households is over $66,790, making the Internet user a very attractive customer for concierge companies to target. Use social media to your advantage. Most educated professional people use the Internet for paying bills, making purchases and more.

Internet Users in the World
Distribution by World Regions - 2011

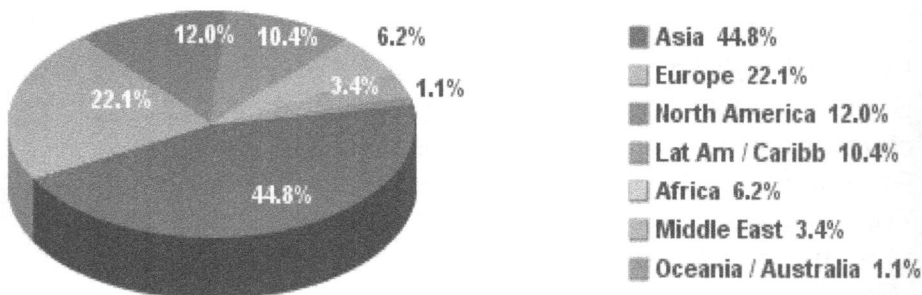

- Asia 44.8%
- Europe 22.1%
- North America 12.0%
- Lat Am / Caribb 10.4%
- Africa 6.2%
- Middle East 3.4%
- Oceania / Australia 1.1%

Source: Internet World Stats - www.internetworldstats.com/stats.htm
Basis: 2,267,233,742 Internet users on December 31, 2011
Copyright © 2012, Miniwatts Marketing Group

Statistics show 405 people per minute are on Facebook a great social media to get word of mouth advertising.

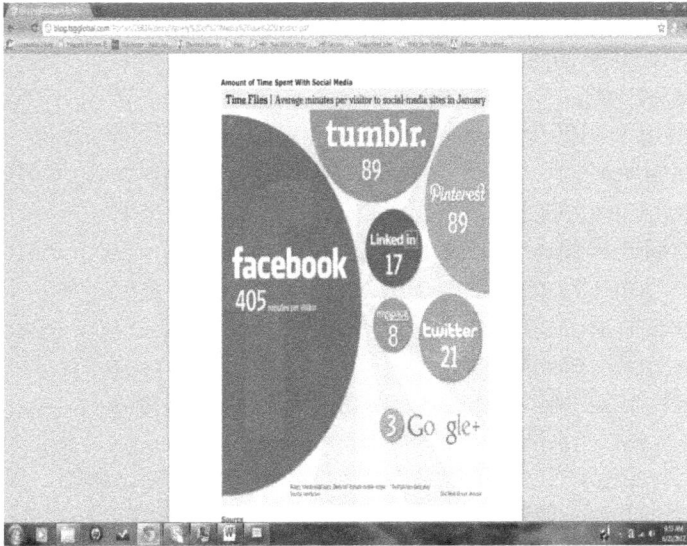

Amount of Time Spent With Social Media
Time Flies | Average minutes per visitor to social-media sites in January

tumblr. 89
Pinterest 89
Linked in 17
facebook 405 minutes per visitor
myspace 8
twitter 21
3 Go gle+

Typically, college-educated Baby Boomers, these Americans try to maintain a balanced lifestyle between high-power jobs and laid-back leisure.
-What companies will compete with you? There are over a thousand concierge services, hotels, and airline industries to compete with.

Step 12 Setting up the office, you will need space for a desk, a file cabinet, a desk top, a printer, copier, fax, and scanner all in one.
Or you can be a Staple's, Office Depot, or Kinko's business person.
There is absolutely nothing wrong with using Kinko's for your copying needs. To avoid procrastination it's a start.
Depending on the size of the project you are doing, whether you own all your office equipment you still may want to use Kinko's.
In this business you will need high speed internet ei. DSL wireless and broadband for fast internet connection and email boxes for sales, orders, customer service and other employee set ups.

A necessity is a good landline phone; clients expect clarity when calling your business.

A good office set up:
• Operating System - Windows Vista, Windows XP, Windows 7 or higher
• MS Office - including Word, Project, and Excel
• Memory - 512 MB RAM or higher
• Web Browser - Minimum: IE 7 with service pack 2
• High Speed Internet Access -
• Monitor -800 x 600 resolution
• Sound - Sound card with speakers or USB speakers
• Instant Messenger - (AIM)
• Anti-Virus Software - Current and regularly updated anti-virus software required (Norton Anti-Virus preferred)
In addition the concierge/ lifestyle manager must have an email account other than a free account such as Gmail, Yahoo or Hotmail. This normally comes with your website hosting package.

• Telephone - Blue tooth and a land line
• Telephone Access - A work phone line (land line only) dedicated to the business
• Toll-free number can make your business appear larger and more professional.
• Faxing Capability - ability to receive and send faxes you can get a fax number at www.efax.com the fax appears in your email.

Business 24/7 should include:
• Phone (Landline)
• Toll free number
• E-mail
• Website
• SMS messaging
• Online chat

Step 13 Get an EIN from the IRS- call the IRS and get an Employer Identification Number or visit IRS.gov complete the ss4 form.

The concierge business will need this number when dealing with almost everyone in government at all levels and with banks, suppliers, vendors, and others.

Step 14 Set up a bank account, Pay Pal account, Apply for a business credit card- your bank will be more than happy to provide you with a bank account. Make sure you have a practical percentage rate. Begin using the card for all your business related purchases. The usage of your business credit card will help your accountant and it will help your company to establish a business credit history. Be wise with purchases and pay them off as soon as possible.

Step 15 Apply for a merchant account, if you are going to take credit cards. Pay Pal in eCommerce has the business of almost every person who does business on the web. Pay Pal has marketing tools such as merchant accounts for accepting major credit cards and you can get a credit card through them.

PayPal is an easy way to take payments. PayPal has mobile capabilities. Square is another merchant account that is trending. It can be used on your iPad, android phone, on the go very small device that accepts Visa MasterCard, American Express and Discover.

Funding for your business
*SBA lenders
*Traditional bank lenders
*Private Lenders
*Venture Capitalist
*and many more alternative financing sources

Marketing the business
Step 16 Register your domain name, try to make it match with the business name, with matching business card. The website can be hosted and cards can be printed by

Vista Print it is a very inexpensive marketing company online. Vista Print will give you free starter cards. Also, put your email address on your card from your new website. Give your cards out and call everyone you take a card from. Follow up, follow up, and follow up. Make every contact count.

Step 17 Create business cards, brochures, and flyers to get the message out, about your new business, some organizations request brochures. Promote yourself with as many advertising mediums as possible. Vista Print can be used for cards, brochures, website creation or you may barter with a marketing company. By providing an excellent service you will generate word of mouth clientele.
Direct mail (Vista print make free cards and your company can get direct mail card mailing very inexpensively)
 Advertise in magazines and sites the affluent frequently read. Start blogging about concierge services.
The magazines mentioned earlier in the book are good magazines to advertise your business in.
Newsletters is one of the tools that 1and1 has. 1and1 has a newsletter wizard; you can send your newsletter monthly, quarterly to all your clients through e-mail. Vertical response and Constant Contact offer trial email marketing. PayPal in Ecommerce has the business of almost every person who does business on the web. PayPal has marketing tools such as merchant accounts for accepting major credit cards and you can get a credit card through them.
Pay pal is an easy way to take payments. PayPal has mobile capabilities. Square is another merchant account that is trending. It can be used on your iPad, android phone, on the go very small device that accepts Visa MasterCard, American Express and Discover card.

Offer a free e-book, you can get some interesting e-books and give them away free for visiting your website.

Newspaper ads: Miami Herald has free advertisement on the worldwide web.

Step 18 Create your website
Most web host has web-statistics this tool let you know how many people have frequent your site on a daily, weekly, monthly and yearly basis. It also let you know where the hits are coming from. Upscale Lifestyle Concierge has Google ad word. The Google have counters and Upscale Lifestyle Concierge website host has the visitor counters and statistics. Websites for less is LRE hosting; this hosting company will host your business as low $5 per year and as high as $8 per year, their website is www.lrehosting.com, 1and1 hosting for a professional package is 29.99 every three months, the website address for 1and1 is www.1and1.com the lowest price the company has encountered is $5.99 per month. Go daddy have a hosting package for every budget. The website address is www.Godaddy.com. Yahoo has an economical website builder. Most hosting companies have wizards to assist you. Upscale Lifestyle Concierge does
A simple websites for $99. You must pay the hosting fees. Call us or email us for more information about setting up a website 888-511-1887, or see the websites Upscale Lifestyle designer have designed.
www.theconciergecorporation.com
www.upscalelifestyleoncierge.com
Choosing a domain name:
You can choose a domain name for as low as 2.99, and as high as 5k. A domain can cost 5k or more depending on the demand for the name. Yahoo, Go daddy, 1and1, and LRE hosting all have inexpensive domain names. A word of advice is to keep your name registered for at least 3 years giving the business time to grow.
Step 19 Create a press release with your local paper and with PR Web to get the word out about your new business. For an example of a good Press release, see Upscale Lifestyle Concierge Press Release visit

http://pressrelease.advib.com/upscale-lifestyle-concierge-service-announces-the-launch-of-its-exclusive-concierge-membership-for-the-most-discerning-clientele-lifestyle-press-release.htm
http://www.prweb.com/releases/2012/6/prweb9602196.htm
http://www.floridafl.org/c-603189.htm
Press Release PR Web is a worldwide news distribution that gets your name out there for the phones to ring off the hook. Remember the clients you want to target are intelligent, computer savvy, and they will read your articles.

Step 20 Get out and find clients. Join the local chamber of commerce and other professional organizations. Place your company name and website in free directories DMOZ.com, Triangle Directory, and some local directories.
Business Week has an affiliation with BizWomen.com the website offer free advertising. The company is Directory M with BizWomen website. Establish a routine for marketing your services create a plan to call up 7 new people every week after going to 2 meet ups per week. Give a speech once a month at business leadership meetings and work that plan consistently. Your business name will ring bells in the other business owner ears.

Advertise for $1 with think concierges.

Sample Membership
VIP Platinum
Customized to accommodate the most discerning client who demands the best
Includes
40 Hours of Prepaid Service
20 Business Referrals
Travel Planning
$17,000 Yearly
$1,500 Monthly
Premium
20 Hours of Prepaid Service
20 Business Referrals World-wide
Travel Planning
$10,000 Yearly
$1,000 Monthly
Prestige Service
10 Hours of Prepaid Service
10 Business Referral World-wide
Travel Planning
$5,000 Yearly
$450 Monthly
Preferred
5 Hours of Prepaid Service
2 Business Referrals
Travel planning
$2,700 Yearly
$225 Monthly
Ala Carte
Services on an hourly basis (2 hour minimum) $50 an hour
Log on to your PC now and type
www.UpscaleLifestyleConcierge.com
Personal/Corporate Membership
We have the perfect Gift! **TIME**
Your Onsite & Online Source

VIP ARRANGEMENTS

(Prepaid Hourly Services)
Personal & Corporate Travel
Vacation Package Plan
Airline Reservations
Luxury Accommodation
Corporate Housing
Chauffeur & Limousine
Nanny/ Senior Services
Theater, Sports, Event Tickets
Relocation Services
Travel Arrangements
Accommodations
Grocery & Personal Shopping
Housekeeping, Senior Care, Chef &
Nanny Service arrangement
Event /Conference Services
Venue Search, Site Selection &
Inspection
Contract Negotiation
On-site Management
Budget Analyst
Party & Wedding Planning
Planning & Coordination
Luxury Accommodation
Guest Accommodation
Special Events
If you don't see, what you want listed. **JUST ASK!**
Our lifestyle managers will make sure your request and
specific needs are met according to your time-frame.

Website www.upscalelifestyleconcierge.com

Terms & Conditions

Family members up to three people are authorized to use the membership.

Prices do not include the item requested, it include the service arrangement, client pay for gift purchased, client pay for incidental cost such as mileage incurred, gift purchases, meeting room, and other items. Client pays a flat fee for concierge membership services.

Upscale Lifestyle Concierge Service account executives prefer as much notice as possible but we can take your reservation 24 hours in advance or in a moment. We will do our best to accommodate emergency requests, although an additional service fee will be assessed at the time of payment.

We will fly into you city, state or country, the cost incurred for flights and accommodations must be prepaid.

Upscale Lifestyle Concierge Service accept request via telephone, fax, email, text or web inquiry. A consultant will contact you to set up an appointment or service.

Upscale Lifestyle Concierge Service prefers advance payment for service.

Upscale Lifestyle Concierge Service accepts cash, Traveler checks, Visa, Master Card, American Express, Discover cards and PayPal.

An invoice is sent to your email with your service request detailed, through Pay Pal. You pay via email invoice.

Sample Letter to vendors
Dear Independent contractor

Lifestyle Managers is a prestigious concierge and lifestyle planner's organization. We want to network with concierges, event planners, and travel specialist with extensive contacts within the United States and abroad. Lifestyle Managers combines personalized services with aggressive marketing in Atlanta, Georgia, Orlando and Jacksonville, Florida as premiere destinations for travel and tourism. Our mission is to save our client's time and make their lives easier and less stressful. We are looking to affiliate with concierges, event planners, errand runners, and travel specialists that operate ongoing businesses with satisfied clients. An independent contractor will NOT be hindered from carrying on his/her respective business Lifestyle Managers may from time to time refer its clients to the independent contractor. In the event that the independent contractor accepts such referral or otherwise provides goods and/or services to Lifestyle Managers client, Lifestyle Managers will pay the independent contractor a mutually agreed upon rate. Normally, we charge a 10% referral fee. As a member of Lifestyle Managers network, the independent contractor must agree to provide the very best in quality services and exceptional client care.
The Independent Contractor will work with Lifestyle Managers client as a preferred client and must represent our high quality standards as they would their own clients.
There is NO COST join our network for qualified businesses. If You Would Like To
Join Our Network, please fax proposal and 3 references (888) 511-1887 ext. 84 or email us at consultant@upscalelifestyleconcierge.com. Visit us online @ www.upscaleclifestyleoncierge.com

This is a sample of a business plan not intended for copying

Executive Summary

1.1 Objectives

To provide an informative website for current and prospective businesses clients and business travelers

To establish long-term relationships with all clients

To promote the website and private client concierge and corporate concierge

To extend the concierge market through networking with business organizations, concierges, and lifestyle management services.

1.2 Mission

Upscale Lifestyle Concierge provides expert knowledge. If you have a question or need a service, we can acquire the means to fulfill the client needs. Our company goal is to exceed our client's expectation by providing a superior level of customer-service.

Our company is built on the principles of providing reliable service.

Our cutting-edge service continues to grow by following trends, improving our standard services and listening to the client.

To be profitable by providing more than we receive

1.3 Keys to Success

The business' keys to success will be to:

Put God first, thus giving 10% of all profit to charity

Provide efficient and consistent superior service to our clients.

Provide expert knowledge to address client needs, whether they need to know (the best restaurants or golf courses in the world, or any other information), or require a service to be performed.

Grow and maintain a superior network of concierge services The website's keys to success will be to:

Focus on providing superior customer service.

Sustain a solid member base with current and future clients.

Review the site frequently to ensure current information.

Company Summary

2.1 Company Ownership

Currently, Upscale Lifestyle is a LLC owned by members there are over one hundred members.

Company Start-up Plan

Upscale Lifestyle will have a relatively low start-up cost. Most of our costs will be attributed to office space rental, purchasing and maintenance of system hardware and software, and advertising. The heavy logistical requirements of providing physical concierge services will be handled through affiliates and vendors who will serve as our primary investors. In place of company ownership in Upscale Lifestyle, we will provide these investors with referral business through direct or indirect means.

2.3 Company Locations and Facilities

Upscale Lifestyle's home office is home-based located in Jacksonville, Florida. This will be an office containing all of the hardware and software for running the website and business.

3. Services

3.1 Service Description

Upscale Lifestyle is a company that provides expert knowledge to companies and business travelers in the Jacksonville/ Miami/Orlando/New York/Atlanta area and world-wide. This is achieved through a network of concierge services with which we maintain relations.

3.2 Competition Description

The traditional concierge service would have several competitors in a market such as Jacksonville/Orlando, we have known direct competition.

These are the local competitors Concierge Concepts, Time Savers, Orlando Concierge, and small private concierges. The traditional competition is local hotels 4 star and better are Upscale Lifestyle expectation is to work with the majority of these companies instead of competing with them. Upscale Lifestyle Concierge is a lifestyle management company more modern than traditional.

3.3 Sales Literature

Upscale Lifestyle Concierge will distribute information on the company website; we also plan to use fliers, brochures, and magazine advertisements. These materials would be distributed in places where our potential clients (businesses and business travelers) could find them in hotel information desks as well as within JAX Airport, MIA Airport and MCO Airport.

3.4 Sourcing

Upscale Lifestyle connects clients with information or services provided by our affiliate network.

3.5 Technology

3.6 Future Services

Reproduce the process repeatedly, by selling material DVD and books on how to start a successful concierge and lifestyle management business.

4. Market Analysis

4.1 Market Segmentation

Upscale Lifestyle targets three primary groups

Business and International travelers in the New York, Atlanta, Miami and Orlando area that are busy professionals who need more time in a day and who live and enjoy life.

CONCIERGE AND LIFESTYLE MANAGER MANUAL

Businesses that wish to provide concierge services for their employees or clients.

Elite client who live life and enjoy life at any expense

3) Upscale Lifestyle will also have publicists to contact concierge services that can be potential members of our network

1) Short Term Plan: (1-3 years)

2) Long Term Plan: (4-10 years)

Education: Bachelor of Science Degree majoring in Business Administration from Jacksonville University and Masters in Business from University of Florida in Jacksonville, Florida

Open Position

6.3 Management Team Gaps

6.4 Personnel Plan

The following table illustrates the Personnel Plan for Upscale Lifestyle.

Specific needs, compensation, and timing is indicated for each position.

Executive	2010	2011	2012
Denise Harvest	$50k	$55k	$70k
Antoine Downing	$50k	$65k	$85k
Desiree Ertuly	$75k	$80k	$100k
Suzanne Jones	$70k	$75k	$95k
Open Sales Position	$ $	$ $	$ $

7. Financial Plan

7.1 Important Assumptions

1) The Internet will continue to grow as a major source for businesses and business professionals to get information and obtain concierge services

7.2 Key Financial Indicators

Income to Upscale Lifestyle will be obtained in the following ways:

_ Concierge Services (50%)
_ Lifestyle management (25%)
_ Hotel and Airline reservations (10%)
_ Car rental (5%)
_ Sold-out Tickets, Events, and Entertainment (5%)
_ Restaurants (5%)

Advertisement/Promotion Costs
Newspaper/magazine 50,000.00
On-line advertisement 10,000.00
Total $60,000.00
Development Costs
Office supplies/furniture 4,000.00
Office lease deposit 1,000.00
Insurance 2,000.00
Host monthly fee 400.00
Total $7,400.00
Hardware Costs

CONCIERGE AND LIFESTYLE MANAGER MANUAL

Server   4,000.00
(5)Laptop Personal Computers 5,000.00
(2)Laser Printers   1,000.00
All-in-One Fax Machine   499.00
 Total $10,499.00
Software Costs
Microsoft Office Windows 7   1800.00
Adobe Photoshop   650.00
Total Startup Costs $12,810.00
Capital
Startup Investments 10,000.00
Employee starting capital 40,000.00
Capital $50,000.00
7.3 Breakeven Analysis
 (Fixed costs/1) - (variable costs/sales)
Breakeven Point: $288,000
7.4 Projected Profit and Loss
Pro Forma Profit and Loss
2010   2011   2012
Sales
Direct Cost of Sales
Other
Total Cost of Sales
Gross Margin
Gross Margin %
Expenses:
Payroll
Sales and Marketing
and Other Expenses
Depreciation
Leased Equipment
Utilities
Insurance
Office Rent
Payroll Taxes
Other
Total Operating
Expenses

Profit before Interest and Taxes
Interest Expense
Taxes Incurred
Net Profit
Net Profit/Sales
7.5 Projected Cash Flow
Pro Forma Cash Flow
Cash Received
Cash Balance
7.6 Projected Balance Sheet
Assets
Current Assets 2010   2011   2012
Cash
Accounts Receivable
Total Assets
Current Liabilities
Accounts Payable
Current Borrowing
Other Current Liabilities
Subtotal Current Liabilities
Long-term Liabilities
Total Liabilities
Net Worth
7.7 Business Ratios
Return on Assets
Current Ratio%
Operating Profit Percentage Ratio %

Sample flier

YOUR solution to a stress free life with MORE TIME TO SPARE

WE CAN HELP MANAGE YOUR TIME BY ARRANGING SERVICE FOR YOUR NEXT PARTY, A HOUSEKEEPER, BUTLER, CHAUFFEUR, MAKE THOSE APPOINTMENTS AND TRAVEL ARRANGEMENTS ON A WEEKLY, MONTHLY OR YEARLY BASIS...WE HAVE A PLAN JUST FOR YOU
VISIT OUR WEBSITE AT
WWW.UPSCALELIFESTYLECONCIERGE.COM
OR CALL 888-511-1887 SO WE CAN MAKE YOUR LIFE MORE ENJOYABLE!

Sample Survey

I would be likely to use a concierge service like Upscale Lifestyles for:

(Check all that apply)

- Personal services, home, auto, pet services
- Tickets to theater, sports, other events
- Travel and vacation planning-including air, hotel and car reservations
- Restaurant reservations
- Information and product-specific or general research
- Gift delivery services, including flowers and gift baskets
- Personal shopping and hard-to-find items
- Personal meeting & event planning
- Corporate, meeting & event planning

I feel that a corporate concierge service like Upscale Lifestyle would

-Save me time

-Save me money

- Make me more productive at work
- Boost my morale at work
- Reduce my stress

-Help with life's important tasks, including personal services and errands

-Demonstrate my employer's commitment to my work life balance

-Allow me access to items I would not otherwise have i.e. Tickets, tables at restaurants, sold-out tickets, gift items, etc.

I would most likely access/contact Upscale Lifestyle as a Service Provider:

(Check the most appropriate)

-Phone

-Email

- Text

-Fax

I expect that I would contact Upscale Lifestyle as a Service Provider:
(Check the most appropriate)
-Every day
- Once a week
-3-5 times a month
-Once a month
- 4-6 times a year
- Not often
- Not at all
Other:

If my employer sponsored Upscale Lifestyle as a Service Provider, I would be willing to pay
Minimal co-pay for services requested:
-Yes
-No
- Maybe
Other Please explain
Name
Address
City/State/Zip
Email address

FAQ for website

What is a Concierge Service?

A French word that means "Gatekeeper", concierge service is a service designed to provide busy people assistance managing their daily personal and professional tasks, or to do lists. Our services help to improve our client's personal and professional lives by giving them back time to focus on the things they would prefer to doing. We operate a personal and corporate concierge, a service often found only in a luxury hotels or resorts. We make the impossible happen for you!

Who can use concierge services?

Anyone who is looking to save time, anyone who desire professional customer service or anyone in search of unique items or information can concierge services. Concierge services are customized to the client's needs and the variety of programs offered cater to busy individuals, business clients, hotel guests, apartment tenants, and visitors to our fabulous country. ANYONE can benefit from concierge services.

Why Should I use a concierge?

A concierge is a luxury. Concierge service providers are dedicated to helping busy people manage hectic lives Concierge service will make your life as simple as it should be. Concierge providers know how hard it can be to juggle work, home, family and friends. The concierge will help you find time for yourself and lead the quality of life that you want.

Who has access to my information?

Your personal information is stored in a secured database. No one can access your information except authorized concierges or lifestyle managers. Your discretion is Upscale Lifestyle Concierge highest priority.

Are there any services that are not covered?

No. As long as your request is legal and ethical we will do our very best to make it happen. Just ask!

How do I know if your company is trustworthy?

CONCIERGE AND LIFESTYLE MANAGER MANUAL

Upscale Lifestyle Concierge Service employees, staff, contractors and vendors must complete a background check, the concierge and consultants are fully licensed, bonded and insured.

How much notice is need for service?

Concierge service providers prefer as much notice as possible but we can take your reservation 24 hours in advance. However, we will accommodate emergency requests, although an additional service fee will be assessed at the time of payment.

How are request made?

Opulent Lifestyle Concierge Service accept request via telephone, fax, email, or web inquiry. A concierge will contact you to set up an appointment or service.

Do I have to pay for services in advance?

Concierge service prefers advance payment for service.

How do I pay for services rendered?

Upscale Lifestyle Concierge Service accepts cash, Traveler checks, Visa, Master Card, American Express, Discover and PayPal. An invoice is sent to your email with your service request detailed, through PayPal.

These FAQ is a website content sample

Here is a sample proposal for medical professionals in medical centers.

Request for Proposal Response for Corporation A
Proprietary Note: This document contains confidential information concerning The Concierge. In accepting receipt of this document, Corporation A is not to make this information available in any manner to persons outside the group.
Corporation A
7777 Main Street
Jacksonville, Florida 32244

Mailing address
PO Box 441154
Jacksonville, Florida 32222
Fax: 904-777-7777 Business: 888-511-1887
PROPOSAL@CORPORATIONATYOURSERVICE.COM

Corporation At Your Service (CA) was established in March 2004 as Town & Country Concierge, LLC. CA is an independently owned corporation earning a reputation from our customers and vendors as a highly professional, innovative, and an integrity-based Corporation. CA also has a subsidiary company Upscale Lifestyle Concierge. Twenty one professionals operate the corporation with higher degrees in learning and professional experience. The loyalty to the agency and our clients is evident in our growth and commitment to providing excellent customer service. More importantly, we are a relationship-based business with a focus on customer solutions, top-notch skills, and total accountability for the services we provide. Our company has enjoyed steady manageable growth since our inception in 2004. Currently, we have twenty one full-time employees and 4 part-time employees. Corporation At Your Service has made a decision to expand the company's services into

CONCIERGE AND LIFESTYLE MANAGER MANUAL

medical centers and hospitals in the Northeast Florida area. This relationship closely aligns with our corporate philosophy and allows Corporation A to have a presence with the best hospitals and medical professionals in the world. Our ownership group plays an integral part in managing clients. Jane Smith Owner/CEO is our Project operations manager. She is on the front-line with our corporate division and readily accessible to the medical staff management team should anything arise that needs special attention. The most important benefit to you will be that our management team is here in Jacksonville, Florida and we are only a phone call away at any time.

As part of our commitment to offer the best service in the industry, we created an online concierge desk. Our concierge desk allows our front-line consultant to refer calls that cannot be completed while on the phone or onsite to the online concierge desk. Items that are referred to the Concierge desk include: calling hotel to make reservations, car companies for special requests, calling airlines for seats or upgrades, getting request for emergency passports and other items that may require additional attention. Our concierge desk enables our consultant to be ready for you, our client, and enhance the level of service that each client receives. This staffing realignment has resulted in a huge increase from our medical concierge consultants. By using Corporation At Your Service, you are employing a staff of professional personal assistants who are customer focused and experienced. CA creates a lasting relationship between staff and patients by facilitating excellence in all services provided and remarkable high standard performance to medical staff and patients. The results are increased patient satisfaction; doctors and nurses are eager to serve the clinical needs of the patients knowing that his/her things to do-list are being handled by a competent staff of concierges. We are making a healthcare impact.

Our guest service programs are designed to help patients and their visitors during a time when assistance is most valuable, allowing the patient to focus on his/her health and their loved ones. The guest program is a patient and visitor satisfaction initiative, as well as an employee retention tool. The healthcare industry is preparing for a large entry of baby boomers requiring medical assistance over the next decade. Baby boomers are a service-driven generation; therefore, they will gravitate toward medical institutions that provide concierge services. The proportion of absenteeism attributable to personal needs has been on the rise almost tripling in 2005, if you do not want your employees missing work to take care of personal business, it would be better to let them take care of some of that business at work with an on-site and an online concierge.

Corporation A will like to set up a concierge desk in the lobby of the hospital one or two days per week and be on call for your hospital staff and patients 6 days a week. Concierge is available 6am to 6pm daily; the company can be reached by phone toll-free

1-888-511-1887 ext. 81

*This is only a sample can be revised to fit your need

Organizational Exhibit A

(Completion time: only 15 minutes)

About Corporation At Your Service

Corporation At Your Service we has over 10 years in servicing clients in the medical and travel industry. Currently, services over 5,000 clients in time saving services. The concierges are a group of dedicated lifestyle managers and we work with an extensive network of service vendor partners. Our primary goal is to save your doctors, nurses, and professional staff time and money by delivering quality services and a wealth of information through one single source-Corporation At Your Service. Let us help you and consider any task done!

What we can do for your medical center:

- Save your medical staff, effort and money

-Just One Call (example: arrange for nanny service, housekeeper, dry cleaning pick up, wait service, travel arrangement and senior care service) Just one call and consider it done!

-Wait for serviceman
-☐Relocation Service
-Participate in new employee (doctors, nurses and management) orientation
-Concierge is a human resource benefit)
-Accommodate visiting doctors
-New mommy service
-Senior TLC service
-Get tickets to sold out events

What we can do for the medical staff is only limited by their imagination...
Here's how the service works:
Hospitals pay a flat fee for the concierge service.
Employees cover incidental costs such as mileage, and employee's pay for whatever items they ask the concierge to purchase for them. For all other staff, patients and visiting medical professional we offer a discounted rate.
See Organizational attachment B.
Let us assist you:
In order for us to provide you with concierge service, we ask that you complete the following:
The Service Planner information will enable us to provide your staff with special service offers and to present a proposal /information for your medical staff unique needs.
Service Planner:
About your Medical Center:
Name of Company/Medical Center
Number of staff doctor
Number of management
Number of nurses
Total
Key Staff members:
President/CEO
President Assistant
HR Director

All Department Heads
Please use an additional page if necessary

ORGANIZATIONAL EXHIBIT B
Price Chart
250-500 $43,000.00 per year
501-1000 $86,000.00 per year
The service can be provided at 35.00 per request
Some hospital clients also make the service available to patients. Here's how the service works: Hospitals pay a flat fee for the concierge service. Employees cover incidental costs such as mileage, and employee's pay for whatever items they ask the concierge to buy for them.
For Northeast Florida medical centers, physicians call in and explain what they need done. Corporation At Your Service provides the service for a discounted rate of $35 an hour or the hospital can pay the annual cost and it works as explained above. (Incidental cost)
Corporation At Your Service
Po Box 441154 Jacksonville, Florida 32222
Phone (888) 511-1887 Fax (904)777-7777
Consultant@UpscaleLifestyleConcierge.com

In conclusion, of starting a solid business in concierge and lifestyle management you must start. You must work consistently and persistently. Business Ownership is freedom to enjoy your successes.
Write you plan and work your plan. A failure to plan is a plan failed. You can achieve in this business. The business is portable all you need is laptop, and a cellular device, a mini copier/printer, iPad, Blackberry technology, wireless access and a client database. You can be on a vacation working your business. This plan belongs to Upscale Lifestyle Concierge. The business letter samples, proposals, and fliers you can create your own and succeed as we did.
Good organizations to affiliate with:

CONCIERGE AND LIFESTYLE MANAGER MANUAL

ICEA International Concierge and Errands Association and NYCPA New York Celebrity Personal Assistant I wish you success with your business to join my network email us at www.upscalelifestyleconcierge.com

About the author

My name is Desiree Ertuly. I am an entrepreneur; I have a master's degree in management from the University of Phoenix. I am a successful business owner. I am a native of New Jersey. I moved to Florida to raise my children after my husband died. I needed Maslows Theory a place of safety and belonginess. I desired a place to raise my children where the crime rate remained low

. Before moving to Florida I attended Rutgers University for business classes. I begin to educate and improve myself to set an example for the two young women. I raised the two young women single handily with customer service employment, a career in corporate America in Financial Service, and a chauffeur business. I completed a Bachelor of Science degree in December 2004.

The first business I founded and operated was Chauffeur Kidz Express and Chauffeur Express Inc.

The business clients were single parents and busy professionals who needed an extra set of hands to get their children to and from school. I chauffeured the youth to after school activities. I received business from families, who moved from the school district, and continued to send their children to the schools. I received business from a local nanny service. When picking up the local nanny clients I used their magnetic sign. The magnetic sign attracted a great deal of attention. The magnetic sign read housekeeping, nanny, referral service and more.

The sign started me to think of a business that I could start in which I would never be bored. The business idea was launched. The name of the business was, "The Housekeepers cleaning and errand service." This business was good, the name changed to Town & Country Concierge, LLC. Town & Country Concierge, LLC was started with a

CONCIERGE AND LIFESTYLE MANAGER MANUAL

friend. Town & Country, LLC specializes in concierge services for busy professionals. While assisting a friend in building T&C, I continued researching the area of interest in the concierge industry I wanted to do, that is how Upscale Lifestyle Concierge was birthed. The business started as a sole proprietorship. The business structure was set up this way to start inexpensively, to get the business occupational license in Florida, and to avoid any procrastination.

I evaluated the skills I had acquired through corporate America, education, and my lifestyle. In evaluating the skills acquired in corporate America, at the Marriott as a front desk manager, in this position I was exposed to many young celebrities and business travelers.

I was employed by British Airways in reservations. The employment was very educational. The education opened my insight to customs, visa requirements, and parts of the world I could never have imagined. I used the travel benefits to travel and learn about this remarkable world we live in. While being employed by British Airways I spoke with concierges in hotels. The concierge called frequently to change reservations, book reservations, locate their client's luggage, and get information for their client. I administered first-class service to Middle Eastern Royalty, African, and European affluent, and many wealthy Americans. I assist CEO's of large corporations in booking trips around the world.

I worked for a Fortune 100 best company to work for Deloitte. While employed by Deloitte Travel Center I made reservations, made hotel accommodation, and car service reservation for business travelers. I had to be detailed oriented to work in the airline industry, and with business travelers. Being detail oriented and organized is a definite criterion for success in the industry. Airport codes, airport visa requirements, different countries visas, and passport requirements are a part of the job in airline reservations. The customs and norms are important. In the concierge, industry details are equally important, as a concierge one becomes

CONCIERGE AND LIFESTYLE MANAGER MANUAL

an information broker. Since, I have been in the concierge business I realize the importance of knowing the airports throughout the world. The importance of knowing the airline industry is an asset .This information has made my business a lot easier. I have had my clients request airline information that saved me the long wait on the phone to the airline to get the answer.

Working for British Airways I have taken payments for $15k for a first class ticket and $13k for a business class ticket and not including holiday accommodations. I have booked reservations in hotels that cost thousands of dollars per night. While, being employed by British Airways my goals were set high and I achieved most of them. I am definitely an extremely high achiever; I remained one of the top airline ticket sellers and offered upgrades on all my sells. I knew that if I could sell these premium tickets to the affluent in the reservation capacity, I could sell concierge service privately to the affluent.

In my personal life on leisure or holiday, I have stayed in 5 star hotels with concierge available onsite. My lifestyle has prepared me for this type of business. I worked in the evening at British Airways and I continued to build my business as a concierge and lifestyle manager during the day. I attended University of Phoenix; for a Master's degree in management, I have a BS degree in Business Administration and Management. While attending school I would do my business presentations in all classes, this prepared me for the business meetings I attend, for the corporate presentations I have to give to Fortune 500 company executives, and I did a great deal of my strategic planning in the classes for assignments. I took several of my classes with MBA students. The student's critiqued and offered suggestions for the business. The class was the next best thing to having a board of advisors. The professors at the University of Phoenix were business owners, and corporate executives I received expert advice from them too. Many students were in management, Presidents, Vice Presidents, and Corporate executives continuing their education. I even had a NFL player in my class. Some students use Upscale Lifestyle for their busy lifestyle. The Project Management class gave me skills in using Microsoft Project for almost every project I embark on. This book is a project, the business website creation was a project, and setting up my office was a project. I manage my client's life as I would a corporation. In my lifestyle management and concierge business, I do project management and business consultant.

It is very important to have a wide range of knowledge information is necessary and important in the personal concierge industry. A career as a concierge or lifestyle manager requires one to be able to find the answer that the client is looking for. One has to be resourceful. People call you for information they lack the time to get themselves. The research of the business was very informative and exhilarating. I searched the World Wide Web for all the concierge and lifestyle management services I could find. I read countless articles on the web and in magazines, I frequented Books a Million and Barnes and Nobles looking for books on the concierge industry. I purchased the book from the Triangle Concierge organization by Katherine Giovanni on Amazon. I spent countless hours at the Small Business Development Center in Jacksonville, Florida. The Center has the Entrepreneur Startup book "How to start a Personal Concierge Service." The book as well as Katherine Giovanni was easy to follow as this book is easier to follow. The book you have read is my countless hours of research, organized into a step by step easy to do business.
I speak success and progress over everyone who read this manual and implement a plan of action.

Some of our vendors we use

CONCIERGE AND LIFESTYLE MANAGER MANUAL

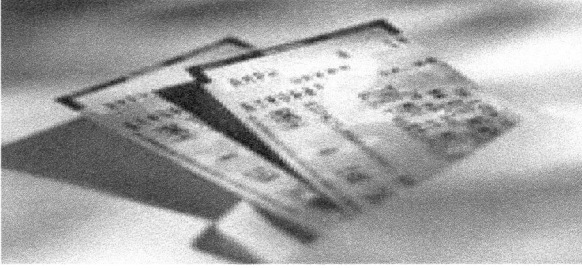

A Place for Tickets
for sold out events
For worldwide corporate service

Airline
Tickets

Affordable
travel tickets

CONCIERGE AND LIFESTYLE MANAGER MANUAL